The Role of Neuro-Linguistic Programming in Enhancing Emotional Intelligence

By Rex Morton

The Role of Neuro-Linguistic Programming in

Enhancing Emotional Intelligence

By Rex Morton

Copyright Page

© 2023 by Rex Morton

This book is a work of non-fiction. Unless otherwise noted, the author and the publisher make no explicit guarantees as to the accuracy of the information contained in this book and will not be held responsible for any errors or omissions.

Published by Omniterra Media Inc

First Edition

Visit the author's website at www.rexmorton.com

For information regarding special discounts for bulk purchases, please contact Rex Morton @ Rex@rexmorton.com.

Disclaimer

This book is intended to provide information about the fields of Neuro-Linguistic Programming (NLP) and Cognitive Behavioural Therapy (CBT) and their potential integration. While the author has made every effort to ensure that the information was correct at the time of publication, the author does not assume and hereby disclaims any liability to any party for any loss, damage, or disruption caused by errors or omissions, whether such errors or omissions result from negligence, accident, or any other cause.

The contents of this book should not be used as a substitute for professional advice, diagnosis, or treatment. The reader should always consult with a qualified healthcare provider about any mental health concerns or conditions. Never disregard professional psychological or medical advice or delay in seeking it because of something you have read in this book.

The views expressed in this work are solely those of the author and do not necessarily reflect the views of the publisher, and the publisher hereby disclaims any responsibility for them.

The inclusion of websites, links, or references to other resources does not mean that the author or the publisher endorses the information the organization or website may provide or recommendations it might make. Furthermore, the author does not guarantee the accuracy of the information these resources provide.

The use of any information provided in this book is solely at your own risk.

In the grand theater of human interaction, language plays a pivotal role. More than a mere medium of communication, language is a powerful tool for influencing thoughts, emotions, and behavior. The genesis of this book lies in this fascinating interplay between language and human cognition and its potential for enhancing one of our most fundamental skills — emotional intelligence.

"Mind Speak: Neuro-Linguistic Programming and Its Impact on Emotional Intelligence" aims to explore this nexus. The objective is twofold. Firstly, to provide a comprehensive understanding of emotional intelligence (EI) and neuro-linguistic programming (NLP), shedding light on their origins, principles, and implications. Secondly, the book seeks to elucidate the potential of NLP techniques to augment EI, offering a practical guide for readers who wish to harness these tools in their personal and professional lives.

The motivation to pen this book comes from my personal journey. As a corporate trainer and a life coach, I have always been intrigued by the potential of the human mind and how we can refine and develop our cognitive and emotional abilities. When I first came across NLP, it resonated deeply with my belief in the power of self-improvement. Through NLP, I discovered a methodology to align our language and thought patterns with our goals, thereby influencing our emotional states and outcomes.

One anecdote that stands out is from an early stage in my career when I was working with a client dealing with profound social anxiety. Conventional approaches seemed to have a limited impact. However, when we began implementing NLP techniques, the change was remarkable. Through modifying her internal dialogue and belief system, she was able to not only manage her anxiety but thrive in social situations. This transformation ignited in me the desire to delve deeper into the realm of NLP and its application for emotional intelligence.

This book, however, is not just about theory. It's a practical exploration of the methods that can lead to enhanced self-awareness, empathy, emotional regulation, motivation, and social skills. It is my sincere hope that by sharing my experiences, the research I have encountered, and the lessons I have learned, this book will enable you to embark on your journey of enhanced emotional intelligence.

As we journey together through the pages of this book, my invitation to you is to keep an open mind. Be willing to question, to explore, and most importantly, to apply what you learn. Because it is through application that knowledge truly transforms into wisdom.

Welcome to "Mind Speak: Neuro-Linguistic Programming and Its Impact on Emotional Intelligence". It's time to unlock the power of your mind and emotions.

In the realm of personal development and psychology, two concepts have surfaced in the last few decades that have significantly impacted our understanding of human behavior and potential. These are Emotional Intelligence (EI) and Neuro-Linguistic Programming (NLP). This chapter aims to provide a primer on these concepts, laying the groundwork for the rest of the book.

In the early 1990s, psychologists Peter Salovey and John D. Mayer coined the term "emotional intelligence," which was later popularized by science writer Daniel Goleman. It is defined as the capacity to recognize, use, and regulate our own emotions in constructive ways to reduce stress, improve communication, empathize with others, face challenges, and diffuse conflict. It also affects how we perceive and comprehend the emotions of others.

On the other side, Neuro-Linguistic Programming, developed by Richard Bandler and John Grinder in the 1970s, is a psychological strategy that entails studying the tactics employed by successful people and using them to accomplish a personal objective. It links ideas, words, and behavioral patterns acquired via experience to certain results.

While EI deals with the 'what'—the understanding and management of emotions, NLP focuses on the 'how'—the patterns and techniques we can use to influence our thoughts and emotions.

The concept of emotional intelligence developed over time as psychologists began to realize that traditional measures of intelligence, such as IQ, were insufficient in predicting success in life. Studies showed that individuals with average IQs outperformed those with the highest IQs 70% of the time. This anomaly threw a massive wrench into the broadly accepted notion that IQ was the sole determinant of success. Further research led to the realization that emotional intelligence was an equally, if not more critical, component of success in life.

Neuro-Linguistic Programming has its roots in the therapeutic work of family therapist Virginia Satir, Gestalt therapist Fritz Perls, and hypnotherapist Milton Erickson, whose techniques were observed and replicated by Bandler and Grinder. NLP was born out of the question: "What makes the difference between somebody who is merely competent at any given skill, and somebody who excels at the same skill?" Bandler and Grinder sought to find patterns of excellence to enable others to perform similarly.

Understanding the origins and definitions of EI and NLP sets the stage for the exploration that lies ahead. As we delve deeper into these topics in subsequent chapters, we will see how these seemingly disparate concepts intersect and how they can be harnessed to improve not only our own lives but also our interactions with others. The exciting journey of unveiling the power of our minds and emotions has just begun.

To navigate the vast ocean of human emotions, we need a compass that can help us identify, understand, and manage these complex internal states. This compass is what we term as Emotional Intelligence (EI).

Emotional intelligence is much more than being "in touch" with your emotions. It encompasses a wide array of skills and competencies that are integral to our ability to succeed in life, both personally and professionally.

Daniel Goleman, who played a critical role in popularizing EI, has outlined five key components of Emotional Intelligence:

Self-Awareness: This is the ability to recognize and understand our own emotions and how they affect our thoughts and behavior. Self-aware individuals are conscious of their emotional states and can identify their emotional strengths and weaknesses.

Self-Regulation: This involves the ability to manage, control, and adapt emotions, depending on the situation. Self-regulation enables individuals to express their emotions appropriately and helps in mitigating impulsive behavior.

Motivation: This component of EI is about being driven to achieve personal or group goals. Motivated individuals display a high level of energy, commitment, and are willing to persevere in the face of obstacles.

Empathy: Empathy involves understanding the emotions of others and responding appropriately. Empathetic people are skilled at recognizing the emotional needs and concerns of others, fostering strong interpersonal relationships.

Social Skills: This involves the ability to manage relationships and build networks. Individuals with strong social skills are effective at leading, managing conflicts, collaborating, and influencing others positively.

Understanding and developing these five components of EI can have numerous benefits in our personal and professional lives.

Research suggests that high EI can lead to better mental health, job performance, leadership skills, and interpersonal relationships. It also plays a significant role in reducing stress levels and promoting overall well-being.

But how can one assess their level of emotional intelligence? Various EI assessment tools and tests have been developed by psychologists over the years. Some of these include the Emotional Intelligence Appraisal, EQ-i 2.0, and the Mayer-Salovey-Caruso Emotional Intelligence Test (MSCEIT). These tools can provide insights into an individual's emotional intelligence and highlight areas of strength and improvement. Keep in mind, though, that these assessments are merely tools for guidance and self-awareness and should not be used as definitive measures of one's capabilities.

By deepening our understanding of emotional intelligence and working to enhance it, we equip ourselves with a potent tool that can dramatically transform our interactions with the world. In the next chapter, we will explore another powerful tool in our journey towards personal development - Neuro-Linguistic Programming.

Changing our thoughts and behaviors can help us reach our goals, according to the psychological method known as Neuro-Linguistic Programming (NLP), which combines the three factors that have the most influence on how humans see the world: neurology, language, and programming. This chapter delves into the science and psychology behind NLP, its fundamental principles, techniques, and also addresses some critiques of the methodology.

At the core of NLP are a set of fundamental principles. The first of these is the idea that our subjective experience of the world, constructed through our senses, is not an exact representation of the world itself, but rather a map that we create. This principle is embodied in the well-known NLP maxim: "The map is not the territory."

The second key principle is that the words we use influence our mental states. The language patterns we habitually use can limit or enhance our perception of the world, thus impacting our experiences and behavior.

Finally, the third principle posits that all behaviors have a structure that can be modeled. By identifying the patterns of thought and behavior that lead to successful outcomes, NLP aims to "program" individuals to replicate these patterns, thereby achieving similar success.

NLP incorporates a host of techniques and strategies, including anchoring, reframing, modeling, and the use of metaphor. For example, 'anchoring' involves associating a particular physical touch or visual cue with a desired emotional state, which can then be "triggered" at will. 'Reframing' involves changing the way one perceives an event, thereby changing its emotional impact.

The science and psychology behind NLP lie in its roots in cognitive-behavioral therapy, family therapy, and hypnotherapy, among other disciplines. The techniques used in NLP are designed to interrupt and change habitual thought and behavior patterns to produce more favorable outcomes. The practice borrows from several established fields of psychological research and therapy, incorporating them into a cohesive system.

However, like any field, NLP is not without its critiques and counter-arguments. Critics argue that the scientific evidence supporting NLP's effectiveness is sparse and that its underlying principles are often too vague to be testable in a rigorous scientific manner. Some also argue that NLP training programs vary widely in quality, leading to inconsistent practices and results. These critiques remind us of the importance of maintaining a balanced view and not blindly accepting any approach without critical analysis.

Understanding NLP and its techniques provides another toolkit for personal development. When used with awareness and integrity, these tools can complement emotional intelligence and facilitate personal growth. As we proceed, we'll explore the connection between NLP and Emotional Intelligence and the potential synergies that can arise from their interaction.

The connection between Neuro-Linguistic Programming (NLP) and Emotional Intelligence (EI) lies in their shared goal: enhancing our ability to understand and manage our emotions and behavior. This chapter will analyze the correlation between these two concepts, discuss how NLP can potentially enhance EI, and explore hypothetical case studies that illustrate their interplay.

NLP and EI intersect in the manner that they both address self-awareness, self-regulation, and empathy. Self-awareness forms the foundation for NLP and EI alike; recognizing our emotions and understanding their impact is crucial for managing our responses. In this context, NLP techniques, like the 'Meta Mirror,' can help individuals understand their reactions to different situations, enhancing self-awareness.

Self-regulation is another common theme. NLP offers tools to manage our emotional states. For example, 'reframing' allows us to change our interpretation of an event, thereby altering the associated emotional response. Similarly, 'anchoring' enables us to associate certain states with specific triggers, providing a degree of control over our emotions. These techniques align well with the self-regulation aspect of EI.

Finally, both concepts highlight the importance of empathy. NLP's concept of 'Perceptual Positions' encourages seeing the world from another person's perspective, a practice that enhances empathy.

To further illustrate the interplay between NLP and EI, let's consider a few hypothetical case studies:

Jane, a team leader, struggles with managing conflicts within her team. She has a high level of self-awareness and understands that her approach might be contributing to the issue. Jane decides to use NLP techniques to alter her behavior. Through 'reframing,' she changes her perception of conflicts from 'problems' to 'opportunities for growth.' This shift in perspective, coupled with an understanding of her emotions (EI), results in a positive change in her team dynamics.

John, a high school student, battles anxiety before examinations. He is aware of his anxiety (indicating EI), but lacks tools to manage it. By learning NLP, John uses 'anchoring' to associate a calm state of mind with a particular trigger - a deep breath. Before examinations, John takes a deep breath, triggering the calm state and reducing his anxiety.

Sara, a therapist, often finds it difficult to understand her patients' issues. She decides to improve her empathy (an aspect of EI) using NLP. Sara uses the 'Perceptual Positions' technique to imagine herself in her patients' positions. This practice enhances her understanding of their emotions, improving her therapeutic effectiveness.

These cases highlight how NLP techniques, used in conjunction with an understanding of EI, can bring about tangible improvements in various life scenarios. The next chapters will delve into how we can practically apply these concepts and techniques to enhance our Emotional Intelligence.

Chapter 5: Techniques of NLP to Boost Emotional Intelligence

In the pursuit of boosting Emotional Intelligence (EI), several Neuro-Linguistic Programming (NLP) techniques can prove incredibly beneficial. This chapter will explore some of these techniques in detail, providing practical exercises and examples to facilitate understanding and application.

Anchoring: This NLP technique involves creating a trigger (or an 'anchor') for a specific emotional state. Anchors can be any stimulus that we can perceive through our senses. To boost EI, you can create an anchor for a calm and focused state, which you can then trigger in stressful situations.

Exercise: Think of a time when you felt particularly calm and focused. Immerse yourself in that memory. As the feeling peaks, create your anchor—perhaps a specific touch, like pressing your thumb and index finger together. Repeat the process a few times to strengthen the anchor. Now, whenever you're feeling stressed or anxious, trigger this anchor to help you return to a calm and focused state.

Reframing: This technique involves changing the way you perceive an event, thus changing its emotional impact. Reframing is particularly useful for enhancing the EI components of self-awareness and self-regulation.

Exercise: Think of a situation that usually causes you stress or anxiety. Now, try to reframe it by finding a positive angle. For instance, if public speaking makes you anxious, reframe it as an opportunity to share your knowledge and engage with others.

Perceptual Positions: This technique encourages seeing a situation from different perspectives, fostering empathy. There are three main perceptual positions: first (self), second (another person), and third (an observer).

Exercise: Think of a recent disagreement you had with someone. First, recall the situation from your own perspective. Next, try to experience the situation from the other person's viewpoint. Finally, imagine observing the situation as a neutral third party. This exercise can help you understand others' emotions better and manage interpersonal relationships, crucial components of EI.

Swish Pattern: This technique is designed to help change unwanted behaviors or reactions. It involves replacing an undesirable emotional response with a more beneficial one, thus promoting self-regulation.

Exercise: Visualize a situation that triggers an unwanted emotional response. Next, visualize your desired response to the same situation. Now, rapidly replace the image of the undesired response with the image of the desired response. 'Swish' between these two images several times until your mind automatically shifts to the desired response.

By incorporating these NLP techniques into daily life, individuals can significantly enhance their EI. Remember that these techniques require practice and patience, so do not be discouraged if immediate changes are not evident. With persistence and commitment, NLP can be a powerful tool in your Emotional Intelligence toolkit.

Understanding the principles and techniques of Neuro-Linguistic Programming (NLP) and Emotional Intelligence (EI) is the first step. The next, and perhaps most critical, is effectively applying this knowledge in daily life. This chapter provides a step-by-step guide to implementing NLP to enhance EI, discusses how to monitor progress, and presents hypothetical case studies and success stories.

Step 1: Self-Reflection and Baseline Assessment: Begin by reflecting on your emotional strengths and areas of improvement. You might consider taking a reputable Emotional Intelligence assessment to establish a baseline of your current EI level.

Step 2: Setting Goals: Once you understand your current state, set specific, measurable, achievable, relevant, and time-bound (SMART) goals for improving your EI. For example, "I will practice the 'anchoring' technique every day for a month to reduce stress."

Step 3: Learning and Practicing NLP Techniques: Dedicate time to learning and practicing the NLP techniques discussed in the previous chapter. Start with one technique, and once you are comfortable with it, move on to the next.

Step 4: Applying Techniques in Real-Life Scenarios: Begin applying these techniques in your daily life. For instance, practice 'reframing' in stressful situations or use 'anchoring' to maintain calm during important meetings.

Step 5: Review and Adjust: Continue to monitor your development. If a tactic isn't producing the desired results, change your strategy or try a different one.

Monitoring progress is as crucial as the practice itself. Keep a journal to record your experiences and emotions, and review it periodically to understand your progress. Moreover, remember that EI improvement is a gradual process. Small, consistent progress is preferable to rapid, unsustainable change.

Let's explore a few **hypothetical case** studies to demonstrate the potential impact of applying NLP for enhanced EI:

Hypothetical Case Study - Alice, a Sales Manager: Alice often struggled with maintaining her composure during high-pressure negotiations, negatively impacting her performance. After learning about NLP, Alice started practicing the 'anchoring' technique daily. She created an anchor for a calm, confident state and used it during her negotiations. Over time, Alice noticed a significant improvement in her composure and negotiation outcomes.

Hypothetical Case Study - Mark, a School Counsellor: Mark found it difficult to empathize with some of his students, impacting his effectiveness as a counsellor. He started practicing the 'perceptual positions' technique to understand the students' perspectives better. As a result, Mark's empathy improved, and he was able to provide more effective guidance.

These success stories illustrate the transformative power of combining NLP techniques with Emotional Intelligence. By consistently applying these practices, you can enhance your EI, leading to better interpersonal relationships, improved mental health, and increased success in personal and professional endeavors.

While Neuro-Linguistic Programming (NLP) can be a powerful tool for enhancing Emotional Intelligence (EI), implementing it effectively is not without challenges. This chapter identifies some common barriers to effective NLP practice and provides strategies to overcome these hurdles.

Lack of Consistent Practice: Consistent practice is key to mastering NLP techniques and witnessing improvement in EI. However, maintaining consistency can be challenging, especially when immediate results are not visible.

Solution: Set a regular schedule for NLP practice, and try to stick to it as much as possible. Use reminders or alarms to keep you on track. Remember that small, regular practices are more effective than sporadic, lengthy sessions.

Skepticism and Negative Beliefs: Some people may be skeptical about NLP or hold negative beliefs about its effectiveness. Such skepticism can act as a barrier to fully embracing and benefiting from NLP techniques.

Solution: Educate yourself about the principles of NLP and the research supporting its effectiveness. Keeping an open mind and being willing to try new approaches are crucial for personal growth and development.

Difficulty in Applying Techniques in Real Life: Understanding NLP techniques theoretically is one thing; applying them in real-life situations is another. Many people struggle to use these techniques when they are in the throes of strong emotions.

Solution: Start by applying NLP techniques in low-stakes situations. As you get more comfortable and see the benefits, gradually start using them in more emotionally charged situations.

Lack of Guidance or Support: NLP can be complex, and learning it without proper guidance can be challenging. Moreover, having support from others can be motivating and make the learning process more enjoyable.

Solution: Consider seeking a mentor or joining a group of people who are also learning NLP. Shared learning experiences can provide support, motivation, and valuable insights.

Unrealistic Expectations: Some people might expect NLP to be a magic solution that can solve all their emotional challenges overnight. When these unrealistic expectations are not met, they may become discouraged and stop practicing.

Solution: Understand that NLP is a tool, not a magic wand. Improving EI takes time and consistent effort. Set realistic expectations and celebrate small victories along the way.

Navigating these challenges may require some patience and persistence, but remember, the benefits of enhancing your EI through NLP can be transformative. As you continue to learn and grow, the hurdles you face will become stepping stones on your path to emotional intelligence.

In the corporate world, Emotional Intelligence (EI) plays a crucial role in determining the success of individuals and teams. Further, Neuro-Linguistic Programming (NLP) can be instrumental in improving EI among employees. This chapter delves into the significance of EI in the corporate setting, the role of NLP in its enhancement, and presents hypothetical case studies of organizations that have successfully integrated NLP and EI into their work culture.

The Importance of EI in the Corporate World: EI is becoming more and more understood as a crucial component of success in the workplace. Better teamwork, stronger leadership, better decision-making, and greater perseverance in the face of adversity can all result from having high emotional intelligence. Higher overall EI levels are associated with lower employee churn, more work satisfaction, and better performance in organizations.

The Role of NLP in Improving EI Among Employees: NLP provides a set of tools and techniques that can help individuals understand and manage their emotions more effectively, thereby improving EI. Training programs incorporating NLP can equip employees with better communication skills, enhance their understanding of themselves and others, and empower them to manage their emotional responses.

Now let's consider some hypothetical case studies of organizations successfully integrating NLP and EI into their work culture:

Hypothetical Case Study – Company 1: Company 1., a leading software company, recognized that its highly technical workforce needed to develop their EI for better team collaboration. The company initiated an NLP-based training program focused on 'reframing' and 'perceptual positions.' This initiative helped employees handle disagreements more constructively and fostered a more empathetic work culture, leading to an increase in overall team performance.

Hypothetical Case Study – Company 2: Company 2, faced with high employee burnout rates among its healthcare professionals, decided to implement a program to enhance EI through NLP. By teaching techniques like 'anchoring,' they empowered their staff to better manage their stress levels. Post-implementation, they recorded a significant reduction in burnout rates and an improvement in patient care.

These cases highlight the transformative potential of NLP and EI in the workplace. By investing in the EI development of their employees, organizations can foster a more harmonious, productive, and resilient work environment. The techniques and principles discussed throughout this book can serve as a guide for individuals and organizations alike in their journey towards higher Emotional Intelligence.

Despite the potential benefits of Neuro-Linguistic Programming (NLP) and Emotional Intelligence (EI), both fields have been subjects of criticism and controversy. This chapter delves into these criticisms, explores their validity and potential biases, and discusses future directions in NLP and EI research.

Criticisms and Controversies Surrounding NLP and EI:

NLP Criticisms: Critics often argue that NLP lacks robust empirical evidence supporting its efficacy. Some view it as pseudoscientific, with techniques based more on anecdotal evidence than rigorous research. Moreover, there is criticism of the commercialization of NLP, with claims that it has been marketed as a cure-all solution.

EI Criticisms: EI has been critiqued for its ambiguity as a concept, with different models defining it differently, leading to confusion. Critics also contend that EI overlaps significantly with personality traits and may not be a distinct intelligence.

Moreover, some argue that an excessive focus on EI might undervalue cognitive abilities.

Validity and Potential Biases of These Criticisms:

NLP Criticisms: While it is true that NLP could benefit from more rigorous research, dismissing it entirely due to a lack of empirical evidence might be premature. Many practitioners report significant benefits, and there are studies that provide support for certain NLP techniques. The commercialization criticism is valid and underscores the need for consumers to critically evaluate NLP services and providers.

EI Criticisms: Although EI's definition varies across models, its core components—such as the ability to understand and manage emotions—are widely recognized as valuable. The overlap with personality traits does not necessarily negate EI's usefulness; it could indicate a need for more refined measurement tools. Finally, promoting EI is not about undervaluing cognitive abilities, but about recognizing that emotional skills are also crucial for success.

Future Directions in NLP and EI Research:

For NLP, future research could focus on empirically validating specific techniques, possibly through randomized controlled trials. It would also be helpful to standardize NLP training programs to ensure consistency and quality.

In terms of EI, future research could aim to refine the definition and measurement of EI and explore its interaction with other constructs such as personality and cognitive abilities. There is also room for more longitudinal studies examining the impact of EI on various life outcomes.

Despite the criticisms and controversies, the potential benefits of NLP and EI for personal and professional development cannot be overlooked. Both fields offer valuable tools and techniques for understanding and managing our emotional lives. By engaging critically with these concepts, we can glean valuable insights that can contribute to our growth and well-being.

Neuro-Linguistic Programming (NLP) and Emotional Intelligence (EI) have become influential fields within personal and professional development over the past decades. Looking ahead, they promise to continue shaping our understanding of human potential and our approaches to self-improvement. This chapter explores predictions for the future of NLP and EI in personal and professional development and highlights emerging trends and potential future research.

Predictions for the Future of NLP and EI in Personal and Professional Development:

Increasing Importance of EI in the Workplace: As workplaces continue to appreciate the significance of 'soft skills,' EI is likely to become an even more sought-after competency. Companies may invest more heavily in EI training and assessment as part of their employee development programs.

Wider Use of NLP in Various Domains: The versatility of NLP techniques could see them being adopted in various areas beyond personal development, such as education, healthcare, and even technology. For instance, NLP techniques could be used in schools to help students manage stress, in healthcare to support patient recovery, and in technology to enhance user experiences.

Greater Integration of NLP and EI: Given that NLP offers practical tools for enhancing EI, we can expect to see greater integration of these two fields. This might involve more NLP-based EI training programs and research exploring the efficacy of specific NLP techniques for boosting EI.

Emerging Trends and Potential Future Research:

Digital EI and NLP Training: With the rise of digital technology and remote work, we might see more online platforms offering EI and NLP training. This could make these tools more accessible to people around the world.

The Role of EI and NLP in Mental Health: Given the increased global focus on mental health, future research might explore how EI and NLP can support mental well-being. For instance, research could investigate the effectiveness of NLP techniques in managing mental health conditions like anxiety or depression.

The Neuroscience of NLP and EI: As neuroscience advances, we may gain more insight into the brain mechanisms underlying NLP and EI. This could provide a deeper understanding of why certain techniques work and how to optimize them.

NLP and AI: As artificial intelligence becomes more advanced, there might be potential to incorporate NLP principles to make AI more 'emotionally intelligent.' This could revolutionize areas like customer service and healthcare.

The future of NLP and EI holds exciting possibilities. By continuing to explore and refine these concepts, we can unlock greater potential for human growth, personal satisfaction, and professional success.

As I sit down to pen these final thoughts and personal reflections, I am filled with a sense of gratitude and anticipation. Throughout my journey with Neuro-Linguistic Programming (NLP) and Emotional Intelligence (EI), I have been continually amazed at the transformative power these tools have—not only on myself but on countless others.

When I began my exploration into NLP, I was initially skeptical. Like many, I questioned its scientific basis and the grand claims associated with it. However, as I delved deeper and began to practice the techniques myself, I started noticing subtle shifts. My interactions with others became more empathetic, my understanding of my emotions deepened, and my reactions to stressful situations became more measured.

Applying NLP to enhance my EI was not an overnight miracle, but a journey. A journey marked with moments of insight, occasional frustrations, and gradual transformation. Over time, I found myself navigating the highs and lows of life with greater ease and resilience. Relationships improved, professional challenges seemed less daunting, and overall, life felt richer and more meaningful.

Through this book, my aim has been to share the knowledge and insights I've gained from my experiences and study of NLP and EI. It is my firm belief that these tools, despite their criticisms, offer invaluable resources for personal and professional development.

The journey to emotional intelligence is not a destination, but a continual process of growth, understanding, and change. It requires practice, patience, and persistence. However, the rewards are profound. From improved relationships to increased well-being, and enhanced professional success, the benefits are manifold.

As we step into an era where soft skills like empathy, self-awareness, and emotional regulation are increasingly valued, the role of tools like NLP and EI in personal development becomes more prominent. It is my hope that this book serves as a helpful guide on your journey toward enhanced Emotional Intelligence.

In conclusion, remember that the journey to self-improvement is as unique as each individual. There is no one-size-fits-all approach. As you navigate your path, remember to keep an open mind, be patient with yourself, and cherish the process.

I wish you the best on your journey. May it be filled with growth, insight, and personal transformation. Thank you for joining me in exploring the fascinating realms of Neuro-Linguistic Programming and Emotional Intelligence.

About the Author

Rex Morton is a renowned author and researcher in the United Kingdom with a passionate interest in the human mind, specifically in Cognitive Behavioural Therapy (CBT) and Neuro-Linguistic Programming (NLP).

Morton has spent a considerable portion of his professional life diving deep into the theories and principles that form the backbone of these two compelling fields. His fascination with NLP led him to complete an extensive certification program, solidifying his understanding of this innovative approach to understanding human behaviour.

Although Morton does not have clinical experience, his intense curiosity and dedication to studying these subjects have made him a respected figure in the field. He has thoroughly researched the integration of NLP techniques into CBT, offering fresh perspectives and insights into how these two methodologies can complement each other to enhance understanding of human cognition and behaviour.

As an author, Morton has successfully communicated his knowledge and passion to a broader audience, making complex psychological theories accessible to professionals and interested laypersons. His writing is characterized by a clear, engaging style and a focus on the practical application of theories, making them relevant to everyday life.

In his personal life, Morton is an ardent lover of the natural world, often spending his free time exploring the British countryside. His passion for landscape photography allows him to capture and share the beauty of these excursions. Despite his accomplishments, Morton is known for his humility and eagerness to continue learning. His work continues to inspire those interested in the intricate workings of the human mind and the exciting possibilities presented by the integration of NLP and CBT.

If you've found the content of this book enlightening and wish to continue your journey of understanding the human mind, I warmly invite you to visit my website at www.rexmorton.com. The website serves as a hub of knowledge where I share my latest findings, thoughts, and insights on the integration of NLP and CBT.

I also encourage you to subscribe to the newsletter available on the website. By subscribing, you'll receive regular updates on a range of topics, from detailed discussions on specific NLP techniques and their application in CBT, to the latest research in the field.

The newsletter is also the first place I'll share news of upcoming releases. Whether it's the announcement of a new book, the launch of an online course, newsletter subscribers will be the first to know. This is a great opportunity to continue learning directly from me, deepening your understanding of NLP and CBT, and enhancing your skills in applying these techniques in your own life or professional practice.

I'm looking forward to sharing this journey with you.